THE ULTIM
INSTAGRAM GUIDE

GROW YOUR ACCOUNT WITH A HIGHLY ENGAGED FOLLOWING WHILE MONETIZING YOUR REACH

First Edition

Table of Contents

Introduction

Welcome, and congratulations on deciding to invest in yourself with our step-by-step guide to Instagram marketing. This book will discuss everything essential for you to start building your Instagram account.

First off, we'll cover the absolute basics on how Instagram started and why you need to leverage the platform for maximum growth and reach. We'll then dive into selecting a niche and strategies you can use to make your profile stand out. Finally, we'll analyze methods to help increase your reach and following while monetizing your account. So, let's get started.

Marketing and Instagram

Instagram marketing is how brands utilize Instagram to connect with their target audiences and advertise their offerings. Right now, Instagram is increasingly gaining fame and attention. Allowing brands to display their uniqueness, interact with clients, discover new partners, and showcase their latest products.

Similar to Facebook and Twitter, everyone who creates an Instagram account has a profile that shows a news feed. Users may socialize together by sharing posts, commenting on or liking videos or photos, and speaking through direct messages, also referred to as DM's.

Instagram enables users to upload videos and photos to your profile and then edit them with numerous alternatives. Instagram has many filters that users apply to increase the appeal of their posts. These preset filters create many changes for photos, for example, adding lighting, giving the image a cold or warm tone, heightening or diminishing saturation, plus far more. Allowing users to edit pictures directly from the platform instead of using a third-party photo editor.

The History of Instagram
Instagram was created by Kevin Systrom, along with Mike Krieger, two Stanford graduates. However, before Instagram became famous as we know it now, Kevin and Mike worked on a location check-in program called 'Burbn.' Later, they decided to scrap the project because of its similarity to four square.

The Stanford graduates didn't give up and instead decided to change their approach. The duo pivoted their effort towards a photo sharing alternative and developed the name Instagram a combination of "instant camera" and "telegram." Instagram was started for iOS on October 6, 2010. After two years of success, the application was developed for Android users on April 3, 2012. Instagram, at that point, had been downloaded more than 1 million times in under a day.

Right afterward, Instagram was acquired by Facebook for about $1 billion. Since the purchase, Instagram has continued to roll out new capabilities. The year 2012 was a significant time for Instagram, rolling out its computer interface later that year.

The site interface has been immense. Yet it's got its functionality limitations as users cannot upload photos on the computer. Nonetheless, it permits customers to scroll through their feeds and view other users' profiles from their desktop computers.

Indeed, one of the features which motivated the chatter and enthusiasm of the app came in June 2013, when Instagram introduced video-sharing for the very first time. Many theorized that it was to contend with Vine, the short-form video-hosting application.

The video feature took off fast and has now become the new playground for previous Vine influencers. In December 2013, Instagram introduced direct private messaging. These messages could be sent through text, photos, or videos and have as many as 15 people in a DM group.

In 2016, Instagram made a drastic change. Instagram substituted its original logo with a brand new and vibrant version. As some of you may remember, the initial logo was brown and beige, resembling an old school polaroid camera.

The logo was changed to what we now instantly recognize and associate with Instagram, the purple and orange camera. However, this wasn't always the case as the new logo took some getting used to; people had to hunt for at least 30 minutes in the app store to find the Instagram app.

Additionally, in June of the same year, Instagram switched from its chronological old-to-new newsfeed into an algorithm-based feed. The shift was published to ensure the content users were visiting was tailored to their previous interactions, thus gaining higher engagements.

While its intentions were pleasant, the shift was met with some serious controversy. The documentary 'The Social Dilemma' sheds some more light on this.

So far as social media marketing channels go, Instagram has become a significant power player. And this is especially true for e-commerce organizations that use visually-focused content to interact with passionate followers and gain higher engagement.

In the last few years, Instagram has evolved and grown at an exciting speed. Embracing new features at an adaptable pace and becoming valuable for users and retailers equally.

In this beginner e-book, we will outline each of the principles for Instagram promotion. These tactics will be up to date as of late 2020, but as these platforms change and adapt, we'll do our best to upgrade the book.

Overview of Instagram Marketing

In social media marketing, Instagram is one of the best tools to grow your brand recognition. If you want to become an online influencer or grow your brand, then there is no way you should be ignoring Instagram.

One of the main areas Instagram can help you with is building a great SEO. If you do not know what SEO is, it stands for search engine optimization, meaning showing up on the top search results on websites like Google.

If you want free, unpaid traffic, the best way to go about it is to rank high on Google. Google appreciates it when a website has many social media platforms connected to it, specifically Instagram.

If you have an Instagram account with a good reach, your site's chances of ranking on Google will be higher. Instagram will not only give you the platform to grow, but it will also give you the free and paid traffic that you have been searching for.

Secondly, Instagram will help you network with many successful businesses and customers. Over the past few years, many people have joined Instagram to connect and network. The reason behind this is; Instagram has over a billion monthly active users on the platform, and it's still growing. You can reach many people online; most of them already have an Instagram account, so why not meet them there? Many people call Instagram a person's online resume, so treat it as such.

Instagram additionally opens a world of opportunities for influencers. You get the privilege of being invited to prestigious events, get sent free products, and offered opportunities to travel. The prospects, of course, depends on the niche you build on. Nonetheless, occasions like this benefit both parties as it helps grow your brand and expose the experience to your followers.

Finally, Instagram can help you with advertising using their ads platform. You essentially pay Instagram to target specific people. Helping you get more exposure, sales, or followers.

Most brands use Instagram ads, and these can be spotted through your feed. To identify these, look out for posts from pages you don't follow. They'll have the tag 'sponsored' underneath their username, signifying they're paid ads.

After reading this book, you will have all the knowledge needed to be successful on Instagram. We hope you take action on the steps we'll go through so you can reap the benefits of leveraging Instagram.

Types of Instagram Accounts

Instagram offers three types of accounts: personal, business, and creator. Picking the type of account you want for your profile depends on your reason for using Instagram.

Suppose you want to use your Instagram profile simply to connect with friends and family and have no plans of monetizing your Instagram page. In that case, the personal account will be best for you. This account is unique as it allows you to set your profile to public or private (meaning that people must send a follow request to connect with you). A personal account leaves out the ability to analyze your following, a feature offered by the business and creator account.

The next profile we will discuss is the creator profile. This type of account works best if you are an influencer, public figure, or content creator. Choosing a creator account can help you monetize your page as you can have your preferred contact details on display, making it easier for brands to contact you. The analytics offered through this account can likewise help you figure out which sort of content most resonates with your audience so you can create more of them.

Finally, the business account, like the creator account, offers unique ways to contact the business and provides valuable insights to better manage and grow the page. Some other features accessible for business profiles are running ads, tagging products with Instagram shopping, and managing branded content.

To switch your profile type, simply head to settings (click the three horizontal lines at the top of your profile page to find this). Next, select "account," and if you have a personal profile, you'll be given the option to switch to a professional account with the preference of either a creator or business account.

Will Instagram Work for You?

As you know, Instagram has over billions of people visiting each month as of January 2020. After being bought by Facebook, the growth increased exponentially. It was mostly a place for people, primarily photographers, to upload their photos when it came out. Now, Instagram is a place where you can connect and grow your brand.

Many of you might be wondering, is Instagram easy to use, and can it be used by a regular person who isn't tech-savvy or photogenic? The truth is that Instagram can be used by anyone who has a smartphone and can take a picture. Meaning that you do not have to be a professional to take advantage of the platform. This is what makes Instagram one of the best and easiest tools to use when growing your brand and getting more recognition. And the most significant part is it's free!

To stay relevant on Instagram, all you have to do is upload good photos consistently. Your goal in posting on Instagram is to engage with your followers, build trust, and offer them products or services they would be interested in.

Whatever you post must be engaging, which usually works with having a call to action. For instance, if you are trying to get more engaged followers, write down in the caption, "what do you guys think? I'd love to know your thoughts" or "do you guys agree?"

I believe in Karma's law, which states that; you get what you give out. So, it's always a good idea to equally interact with your audience by liking and commenting on their posts, building goodwill and trust as you go. We'll touch more on this soon.

Your main goal should be to post content daily, although you can start with two or three uploads a week if this is a stretch. Make sure that whatever you post relates to your brand and the people you want to reach. Posting twice or thrice a week and keeping the content relevant will help you keep your audience engaged. That is an essential fundamental to remember when starting your Instagram page and growing your audience.

Luckily the only device you'll need to grow your page is a smartphone to create and upload content. Most of the time, you can even repost other people's images by simply tagging them in the post. This will help you gain goodwill with them and grow your brand simultaneously.

It Has to Be Both Ways

You must realize that social media involves forming a relationship between a brand and the customers. Hence, having a great engagement rate is vital for building up your social media platform and brand.

Remember, the key to increasing your engagement rate is to stay connected with your fan base. Always reply to them and be helpful whenever you can.

A great way to practice two-way communications on your social media accounts is by acknowledging comments from your audience. You can do this by commenting back with a simple "Thank you." Another way could be by affirming their comments on your posts by writing things like, "We know, right!" or "Spot on!"

The most crucial two-way communication can happen when somebody posts something critical or negative about your brand on its social media account. Never react to it with the same negative energy, emotion, or tone of writing the negative comment was posted.

Instead, take the high road by, first, acknowledging their concern, e.g., saying something like, "I am sorry to hear that" or "I can imagine why you feel that way." You will not be validating their critical or negative comments about your brand or post by responding that way.

In many cases, bashers are disarmed when they hear (or read) that their statements were not easily dismissed. Especially when they see that their opinions were acknowledged, even though they were not necessarily accepted. Doing so also shows your audience that your brand is classy and professional.

A common issue most people have with growing a successful Instagram page is gaining a following. It can be disheartening looking at people who have millions of followers when you are first starting.

From my experience of growing several Instagram pages to thousands of followers, I'll give you a tip. The key is to remember; the journey might be challenging to begin with but will get easier. The tipping point comes when you've reached around 1,000+ engaged followers, post consistently, and use the right hashtags. This will cause your Instagram page to gain momentum, similar to the snowball effect.

To get to this point, I recommend for anyone who sets up an Instagram account to find large accounts in your chosen niche, engage with their content/community, and follow the people you bond with. Some of these people will follow you back and come back to your page and engage with your content. Unfortunately, some won't, so it's a good idea to go on a unfollow spree now and then.

Which leads us to our next chapter: choosing your niche...

Chapter 1   Finding Your Unique Niche

Finding your niche is a vital part of building a successful Instagram page. So what is a niche? A niche is a profitable segment of a market, suitable for your attention. Examples are fitness, business, fashion, baking, and so forth. You can effortlessly identify your niche as there are so many. You can choose one depending on what you like, enjoy, or admire.

Finding your niche on Instagram is essential because you will gain more engaged followers and build a tight-knit community. For example, suppose your niche is health and fitness. In that case, you will have amassed a group of followers trying to get healthy and learn new exercises or recipes. As this is a vast niche, your followers will reach the thousands quicker and easier if you put in the time and effort. You could dive even deeper into this niche and focus solely on recipes or exercises, depending on your preference.

Therefore, now that we have identified what a niche is, we need to understand the basics. The basics of finding which niche is right for you and how to use your niche to your advantage. This is what we are going to focus on in this chapter.

The first step to finding your niche is to identify your interests and passions. This will help you determine which segment is best for you and help you identify what sort of content your potential audience will resonate with.

Identifying your passions and interests may be a step that you have previously considered, that's good. But if you have not, you should produce a list of ten hobbies or passions you care about and enjoy.

This activity will help you figure out what you should focus on. Instagram is not easy, and neither is business or branding. At some point, it is going to get complicated. If you are engaged in a field that you do not have any personal interest in, the odds of you giving up will double. This is notably true if you are doing this for the first time.

Some things to help you decide what your interests and passions are is to ask yourself the following questions:

- Do you subscribe to any magazines?

- What type of books do you like to read?

- In the library, what topics do you want to learn about?

- Do you belong to a club or an organization?

- Is there a specific type of club you would like to belong to if you could?

- How do you like to spend your free time?

- What do you look forward to when you are not doing anything?

- What do you miss when you are not able to do it?

1.	6.
2.	7.
3.	8.
4.	9.
5.	10.

The next tip that you should utilize is to identify a problem that you can solve. With your list of interests and passions, we can now narrow it down to how we can potentially solve a community's pain point. This is ideal if you are trying to create a profitable brand or a business. You need to find the problems that your customers are likely to experience and then determine whether you can solve them. People are also more likely to follow you if they feel like you can solve a problem they have.

Another good tip is to go and look at the discussions that are taking place in forums with your niche. What kind of problems are people having? What are they looking for, and what do you need to do that others cannot do? Join the discussion and make sure that you're creating a framework for asking questions. Asking questions will help you discover if you're on the right path and if it's something you can dedicate your time and effort to.

You should additionally research your competition because the presence of opposition is not always a bad thing. Rivals could show you what you need to do and how you could improve. Is the competition in your niche offering quality? Are they fake, or are they paying people for reviews?

Differentiate yourself from that by being real. Produce real content that is high quality, look for pain points that they are missing, and tailor your services and products to your followers.

You also need to be able to determine the profitability of the niche that you have. Through researching the competition, we should have a rough framework of how much money you have the potential to make. If you haven't yet, it's a good idea to browse the top products in the category you have chosen for yourself. For example, suppose you decide to go into the yoga niche. In that case, it's great to identify what sort of products people in this niche purchase. Look for the major brands and see how many people usually tag them in pictures and how often. The follower count can also be a good indication of how many of their followers purchase their services. As a rule of thumb, it's usually around 5% of the audience.

If you cannot find any offers, then that could be a bad sign. It might mean that nobody has been able to use this niche for their benefit. However, you might be able to succeed where others were not able to capitalize.

If your search does turn up a good number of products but not an overabundance, then you are in luck. You might have found a rare gem.

Next, make a note of the price points so that you will be able to price your products or your brand similarly. However, keep in mind that you don't have to have a business or brand with your own product offering. You can also partner with other people, other advertisers, and other influencers in your niche. This will help you generate commissions through affiliate links and sponsored posts etc.

Now that you are armed with the information you need to choose a niche, the only thing left for you to do is test out your idea. Which leads us to our next step, setting up your profile.

Chapter 2   Getting Started on Instagram

Creating your Instagram account is best done on a mobile device, as Instagram has been optimized for mobile usage. While you can still set up your account on the platform's desktop version, it isn't recommended. As it can be a challenge because fewer features are available.

To get started on mobile, you will want to go to the app store and download Instagram. Once the app has been downloaded, you can launch it and follow the on-screen process for creating your account. Once you have done that, the next page will require you to choose a username for your account.

Choosing Your Handle

The Instagram handle that you choose needs to be self-explanatory and easy to remember; otherwise, your audience may not find you. When choosing your username, you want to make sure your username's first impression forms a connection. A connection between who you are and what you do; otherwise, users may not be tempted to click onto your profile page.

In general, most brands use their company names for their handles, making it easy for them to be found on Instagram. For example, Nike, Adidas, Walmart, and Nordstrom all use their brand names as their usernames. This makes it easier for them to be recognized on social media platforms.

Typically, personal brands follow the same rule of thumb as other brands, using their names as their usernames.

Crafting the Perfect Bio

Once you have created your username, the next step will be to write your bio. On Instagram, your bio can be up to 150 characters in length and can include links to other profiles and hashtags that may be relevant to your brand.

Your bio allows people to know who you are and what you are about, though you can also use it to generate leads and market your business. Taking full advantage of your bio can increase your page's memorability, interaction rate and help gain followers. When it comes to writing a bio that will help you make sales, there are three things that you need to focus on: catchy content, being informative, and promotions.

You want your bio to be catchy enough that people are interested in reading it. It also has to be informative so that people can get a feel of who you are and what your company is about. It can also be promotional so that people click on the link you include.

Typically, complete sentences are frowned upon in bios unless you are using a single short sentence, so refrain from using anything too excessive or wordy. In most bios, rather than using sentences, people share lists of their interests or what their brand is all about. Writing a good bio is essential, so be sure to take the time to identify what is going to work for you and your brand.

The best way to get a good feel for what will work for your unique brand is to go to the pages of other brands in your niche and read through their bios so that you can see what works and what does not. Take a look at the bios of successful pages versus unsuccessful pages and see any trends or differences that seem to set the two apart.

You want to model successful brands, so you can attain their level of success. It's a good idea to attempt to recreate the positives in their bios on your account but more authentically so that it resonates with your brand and your unique target audience.

In addition to writing your bio, you will also want to share the link to your website. Allowing people to see more of who you are and have the opportunity to shop online if you have an online store.

Uploading Your Profile Picture

Your profile will require a picture, which will provide your audience with the opportunity to visually see who you are. Cementing the connection between your name and your image.

When it comes to creating professional accounts, you have two options with your profile picture: upload a photo of your logo or upload an image of yourself. Your choice will depend mainly on what type of account you are running and which image you want people to remember.

For most companies, the logo will suffice as this is the easiest way to begin building brand recognition through your business. As people come to associate your logo and username with each other, they will also come to recognize your logo and identify it in other places. This can be huge for brand recognition, so it's wise all companies have their logo as the profile picture.

If you decide to use your logo, make sure that you upload a high-resolution image. Ensure that it fits perfectly in the profile image circle so that your logo can easily be seen.

When branding yourself, you may prefer to use an image of your face rather than your logo. Personal brands typically seek to inspire brand recognition through facial recognition.

Ensure that you use a clear photo that accurately reflects your brand and makes sense with the overall image you are attempting to create. For example, if you are a travel blogger, use a picture of you with an impressive outdoor backdrop to help people make the connection. If you are a real estate agent, have an image of you smiling in front of a home or a blank wall so that you have the emphasis on yourself and your influence as a salesperson.

Do not use selfies, low-quality images, or images that seem out of place in this space. This can result in people feeling confused around your brand, leading to fewer followers and, therefore, fewer sales. You should be leveraging every aspect of your page to create one uniform image that accurately reflects your brand.

Ensure you never leave your profile image empty, as people will not trust or interact with accounts that have not yet uploaded profile images. Refrain from communicating with anyone until this has been done.

Most people who see profiles without images will assume that these profiles are either scammers or not yet interesting enough to pay attention to.

The profiles with attractive, clean, and high-quality enticing pictures are the ones that end up getting followers. So wait until you have filled this in before engaging with people's content or following anyone's profile.

Two-Factor Authentication

Having a two-factor authentication is necessary for anyone who wants to run a business online. It ensures that people cannot hack your account and steal your followers. Getting your account stolen can also create havoc on your brand image if the hacker's intentions include just that.

Two-Factor authentication will require you to approve all new logins, either through your phone number or email address. This means that if anyone attempts to log into your account remotely to hack you, they will not be able to get in without your code.

You can enable two-factor authentication by going back to your settings menu, tapping "Privacy and Security," and then tapping "two-factor authentication."There, you will be walked through verifying either your phone number or an email address you'll use to make your account more secure.

Suppose you receive a request to log in, but you have not attempted to log in anywhere. In that case, it is essential that you immediately change your password on Instagram.

If you received a code, this is proof that someone has identified what your password is and has successfully passed the first barrier of security to your account.

Of course, they will be stuck on the login process since they do not have your verification code to complete the two-factor authentication login. But this still means that your account has been compromised and needs attention.

By changing your password, you can ensure that no one can somehow hack into your account and begin compromising your business through Instagram.

Chapter 3   Choosing Content & Leveraging Hashtags

Content

Now that we've gone through the basics of Instagram, got our profile set up and optimized for our exact niche, it's time to strategize our content game plan.

Our game plan involves using content to increase our reach, which will get people to come back to our profile. Once they see what we post and our bio, they'll want to follow us for more, which will eventually trickle down into some sales.

We use content to expand our reach because not many people will go out looking for our username. However, many people will see our content when we use hashtags, shoutouts, ads, and asking people to tag their friends. Therefore, in this chapter, we'll show you the different types of content you can put out there and how to find high-quality content to either replicate or repost.

The main plan we use for our content is 70% of our content to engage with existing followers and reach new people who want to follow us. 20% of our post will gain trust/goodwill from our followers, posting things like recipes, exercises, or doing giveaways. And finally, 10% of our content will be to generate sales.

We use this format to avoid coming over as too spammy, causing people to unfollow us. However, suppose you've got an Instagram shop on your page. In that case, you can tag your products in each image, making it easier to generate sales.

There are 3 main types of content you can post on your account: photos, videos, and stories. Photos are images that you post on your Instagram profile, videos are self-explanatory, and both stay on your profile permanently. Whereas stories only last 24 hours, however, these tend to have higher engagement rates and can be in the form of a photo or video. If you're looking for high virality, I recommend using videos as these auto play on Instagram, thus are more likely to grab people's attention.

So now, let's talk about a way for you to produce content that works. There are two main ways of getting content for your page: creating content and finding content. So how do you get as many likes/engagements on your posts as possible? My top quote is a simple one but effective it states, "success leaves clues." What does this mean? It means that as long as you copy precisely step by step what content people already liked and engage with, you should get similar results.

Posts that do well can be found by going to your explore/discover page or using hashtags, which we'll get into properly later. However, for now, we'll use them to find viral content.

To uncover content that is golden and not just viral, we have to check the profile that posted the content on the discover and hashtag pages. Usually, accounts with a high following tend to get lots of likes on their posts, which aren't the golden nuggets we're looking for.

We're looking for accounts with a decent following that has a disproportional amount of likes to followers.

A general rule of thumb is 10% of followers like any given post. Anything beyond this number is a post that is likely to do well. For example, if 30% of the followers or more have liked the post, it's a golden gem!

Disclaimer: when using other people's posts, please make sure you tag them, or if you want to go the extra mile, ask them for permission. People rarely do this, but you might want to if you own a big brand and don't want to get sued for copyright infringements.

The alternative to finding golden nuggets and reposting them is replicating them and improving upon them to double the results. When you do this, you can also add your branding and include your products to tag. Anything that can help make the content relevant to your audience is worth creating for yourself.

Hashtags

This section is on the power of hashtags. We can't talk about Instagram without talking about hashtags. The hashtag is the symbol (#) followed by a word/phrase that describes a post. They are an essential part of any post.

When it comes to using Instagram for business, you need to use hashtags to gain more exposure. Even a single hashtag could increase your chances of getting more engagement on your post.

Hashtags are an effective way to drive traffic to your content. People can now 'follow' specific hashtags or search for content using hashtags. For example, using #books will bring up lots of images with books; however, you can narrow your search using #kindlebooks or #harrypotterbooks.

When using hashtags, you must use a hashtag that fits your company, post, and preferably ones that get you traffic. Using a hashtag like #summer or #love can bring you extra traffic. If you run an entrepreneurial page, however, these will not be relevant to you. So, you don't want to use those kinds of hashtags; they are not specific to your brand and won't attract the audience you want.

The more specific you can get on your hashtags, the better you'll attract and engage an audience.

Finding the right hashtags -Modeling
How do you find the right hashtags to use? Again, by modeling the most popular companies in your niche and examining the hashtags they are already using. Don't try to reinvent the wheel. Just copy what other successful companies are doing.

We want to create a list of hashtags and start testing them on all our posts. We'll be able to figure out which hashtags work and which hashtags don't. The more specific you can get on the hashtag, the better test results you can expect.

When testing, you will notice that some of the hashtags will seem to get more followers and likes, while others will not even make a difference to your posts. Therefore, keep track of which set produces the best results as we want to keep using the winners.

You can then create an Instagram post signature and save it in an online list keeper like Google Notes and Evernote. That way, you only need to select, copy, and paste your hashtags on your post. There is a simple hack I like to use for hashtags; this makes the post look more professional. Simply put the hashtags in the comments, and you'll get the same effect without it interfering with your caption.

Searching for hashtags

Searching for hashtags by popularity is a great way to get more engaged hashtags for your post. Instagram usually allows about 30 hashtags per post, and we want to use every one of them.

When you go to the search bar and search for a hashtag, you will see the post count for that hashtag. Your initial goal is to use a hashtag where you can easily rank in the top posts. Keep in mind, you'll also want to use popular hashtags to attract people. The more people are using a hashtag, the better engagement you'll get once you rank.

So, we'll try to balance things out when starting. We'll begin with a low post count, and then as your followers grow and you rank highly on those hashtags, we can commence testing out hashtags with higher post counts.

Initially, a hashtag with under 100,000 posts is an excellent number to begin with. As you rank at the top of these, you can gradually increase it and start using hashtags with more than 100,000 posts. As you start using this strategy, you will see minimal results first. However, as time goes on, you will gain momentum, causing your engagement, reach, and followers to increase.

To find your first set of hashtags, think of any basic word that describes your niche, type it into the search bar, and filter it by tags. Many suggestions will come up when you do this. For instance, if you're in the travel niche, you could type the word travel into the search bar, and the suggestions will follow.

Write down all the tags that have a post count under 100,000, then search for more travel-related words like nomad explore, and adventure. Keep doing that until you have a list of 30 hashtags ready to go. As you start using these hashtags, you can slip in a few popular ones with higher posts count; these will be the ones with the most competition. However, we aim to rank at the top for the lower post counts, and eventually, this will allow us to rank for the higher ones.

Using Trending Hashtags
When using trending hashtags, you must be very careful. While it may be tempting to always use trending hashtags, you do not want to come across as a spammer and get your account banned.

We need to put a lot of thought and consideration into the hashtag that we use. Only use hashtags that will be effective and worthwhile for your brand. Disregard the hashtags that don't resonate with your followers.

Try to be attentive with every hashtag you use, as timing is an essential factor for using trending hashtags. Suppose you capitalize on a trending hashtag on time. In that case, you'll be able to gain higher engagement rates and make your brand more memorable.

If you jump on a trending hashtag too late, you should consider scrapping the post. Because at that point-in-time time, your followers might already be experiencing topic fatigue, and you don't want to seem out of touch with the community.

While you can sometimes use mainstream trending hashtags like Fashion Week or Superbowl to gain broad exposure. You should try as much as possible to use niche trending hashtags related to your industry or your brand.

If your company is in the art niche, use hashtags specifically targeting the art community. You'll be able to increase your popularity among your target audience, resonate with your followers, and strengthen the tie with your community doing this.

These are the ways you can use hashtags for your post. I hope you test these methods out and see which one works best for you.

Using hashtags is one way of increasing your reach. In the next chapter, we'll talk about shoutouts, which are just as powerful.

Chapter 4   Shoutouts & Instagram Influencers

For most brands who begin using Instagram, the initial objective is to get followers and build a community of raving fans who will want to purchase their offerings. However, to develop your following, you must master the ability to increase your post's reach. Thus getting more people to visit your optimized Instagram page. The more people who visit your page, the better your chances.

The ability to increasing your influence is a priceless asset. You can leverage your reach to deliver value, market your products, and ultimately grow your business and profits.

The most powerful marketing strategy you can utilize on Instagram to increase your page's exposure consists of leveraging the power of 'Instagram Influencers.' When done correctly, this can grow your Instagram following fast! Along with driving tons of warm leads to your website or sales funnel.

The process of leveraging an Instagram Influencer's community to promote your post, page, or product is called a 'shoutout.' A shoutout involves sharing a post or merchandise to feature on another page. This is usually with the caption containing some form of a call to action, e.g., "go follow this person" or "go buy this product."

Since the beginning of Instagram, this is one of the most fundamental ways to increase your following and sell your products and services on Instagram without going through Facebook's ad platform.

You simply connect with an Instagram Influencer, pay them to post a screenshot of your page, or share a post with your product. Accompanied by a personal endorsement that encourages people to follow your page or buy your product or service.

The concept of 'influencer marketing' did not originate on Instagram; it is widely used through almost every media type. We've all seen famous people work with brands; an example is Dwayne Johnson A.K.A The Rock featuring and working with Under Armour.

Today, using Instagram Influencers to build a community and drive traffic remains an overlooked and drastically misunderstood strategy by most marketers. Their lack of awareness of Instagram's raw power only makes it easier for people like you and me to take advantage of this fantastic opportunity and begin using Instagram as an asset to launch and grow businesses faster than ever before.

Leveraging Instagram Influencers is remarkably simple. But to understand the fundamentals and the specific, time-tested techniques, we will need to dive deep into the overall strategy.

Whether you are looking to grow your follower base, drive traffic to your website, or accomplish both of these objectives simultaneously, there are multiple free and paid strategies that you can begin utilizing today. So, let's break them down, starting with the free tactics.

Shoutout-For-Shoutout (S4S)

One of the most common ways people build their communities on Instagram is by using a shoutout-for-shoutout or what some people refer to as a share-for-share

(S4S). The way this works is you find a page with a similar follower base (in terms of niche and follower count), and you shoutout each other's Instagram page. You are essentially partnering with another Instagram page intending to tap into their community to increase your brand's exposure and attract new followers.

The process by which you introduce your brand to your shoutout partner's community is effortless and straightforward to execute. You create or use a piece of value-based content that the influencer's audience would benefit from, and they share it.

The branded high-quality visual should come with a compelling caption that entices their followers to visit your page and want to follow you. Make sure your Instagram username is in the first line of the caption to make it easy to view without having the user expand the caption to see it. However, each niche has different things that appeal to its audience, so make sure to use the power of modeling successful posts you notice while on your feed.

Shoutout Groups

Shoutouts groups, or what is also referred to as 'shoutout trains,' leverage the power of a group of Instagram pages to multiply the exposure and engagement for everyone involved.

Essentially, a group of active users will get together and start a 'train' where an individual gives a shoutout to one of the group members, followed by the second person shouting out the first person, and so on. All of this happens within a short time, and it takes advantage of the snowball effect, where you are tapping into a ton of Instagram users simultaneously

You will notice that as you grow your following and work with Instagram users who have massive follower bases, the positive effects compound.

You tap into a broader base of Instagram users, which means more followers for your page. In turn, once your Instagram account begins to grow, you become a more attractive prospect, and people will invite you to join their shoutout groups. It's a self-fulfilling cycle that benefits you as you continue to grow your Instagram following.

Shoutout partnerships and shoutout groups can be a great way to grow your Instagram page. However, they can also be harmful to your long-term growth if used carelessly or too frequently. Remember your followers chose to follow you for YOUR content, not other people's.

Paid Shoutouts

Paying for shoutouts might seem entirely pointless to you, knowing that there are other well-known marketing avenues out there. However, as we previously mentioned, this segment of marketing hasn't been tapped yet. Currently, the ROI for every $1 spent on shoutouts returns an average of $11.69. In contrast, $1 spent on conventional ads returns an average of only $2. This puts shoutouts at an advantage of about six times! Imagine what this can do to boost your results.

There are a few different types of paid shoutouts you can get from influencers. These usually depend on the influencers; however, they tend to offer 3 variations: story posts, timed posts, and permanent posts. The prices for permanent posts typically run higher as influencers don't like to keep these ads up to avoid having their page look spammy.

Choosing an influencer to use for your paid shoutouts involves doing a bit of math to get the most bang for your buck. For example, let's say a user has one million followers; we expect about 100,000 followers to engage with the post. Out of those, we want to see around 15,000 profile visits, leading to 3,000 genuine and targeted followers.

Influencers usually have DM for promos in their bio; while some might not have this in their bio, you'll find some don't mind offering their rates.

Influencers tend to get lots of DM's, some of which might be time wasters, so to stand out, it helps with starting your message with a subject, e.g.:

"*Promo Enquire*

Hey .... (Influencers name)

How is it going? Can you tell me (if you offer a paid promo and) how much would it be for a shoutout to my page?

Thanks"

This should get you through the door, and if you are looking for something more official, you can use websites such as www.shoutcart.com.

Bonus

Here are six ways people are using Instagram Influencers to grow their Instagram following:

1. The Instagram Influencer takes a screenshot of your page and features your last 9 images on their page and in the caption tells people to follow you.

2. The Instagram Influencer takes one of your original posts, copies it, or redesigns it, features it on their page, and tells their followers to follow you.

3. The Instagram Influencer creates their usual branded content but gives you a shoutout in the caption.

4. The Instagram Influencer posts your Instagram name on their story feature and tells people to follow you.

5. The Instagram Influencer does a live video telling people to follow you and pins your Instagram name on a comment while doing the live video.

6. The Instagram Influencer does a video telling people to follow you and posts it to their story.

Chapter 5   Taking Advantage of Instagram Ads

In this chapter, we will teach you how Instagram advertising works and all the vital information around running a successful Instagram ad. Helping you get your content to the exact people you want to target. Let's begin with the essentials.

Limited ad services were first introduced by Instagram when Facebook took over ownership in 2013. However, it only began to provide advertising access to all businesses and brands in 2015.

These brands soon realized that Instagram ads were a huge benefit for businesses. Because Instagram is incorporated with Facebook Ads Manager, brands could take advantage of the enormous resources of user data Facebook offers to advertise directly to their target audience.

Here are a few statistics to drive home the importance of Instagram ads:

- Seventy-five percent of Instagram users act on Instagram ads, like heading to a site or buying a product.

- Instagram's potential advertising reach is 849.3 million users.

In essence, if you are not taking advantage of Instagram ads, you are depriving yourself of a considerable amount of revenue.

What Is the Cost of Instagram Ads?

Depending on your ad objectives, the cost of ads will be unique to you. This is because no two ads are ever the same. However, for Instagram ads, the typical CPC (cost-per-click) is about $0.70 – $0.80. This figure was obtained from an evaluation of over $300million spent on ads. ("Instagram Ad Costs: The Complete Updated Resource for 2018", 2018)

Note that this is just an estimate. You may spend more or less depending on numerous factors like the time of the year ads are set-up, the type of content you promote, and your audience's size.

Creating Ads on Instagram

Now, we will begin looking at how to create ads. For this, we will be using the Facebook Ads Manager, which is a predominant method because of its simplicity. Facebook also offers you the ability to personalize your ads better than you could when using the Instagram app. Below are the steps to create an ad.

Head to the Ads Manager via Facebook

Presuming you already have a Facebook account and logged in, all you need to do is follow this link to get to Facebook's Ads Manager. (www.facebook.com/ads/manager)

Instagram doesn't have an ads manager; you can oversee your Instagram ads via the Facebook ads interface.

Determine Your Marketing Goals

Here, you need to pick a campaign goal. The great news is that the objectives are clearly stated. If you are after additional traffic, select the traffic goal. If you want more engagement, choose the engagement goal, and so on.

However, there are only a few goals you can work with using Instagram ads, which include:

- Traffic
- Engagement
- Brand awareness
- Conversions
- Video Views
- App Installs
- Reach

Determine your Target Audience

After determining your objective, you must target the right audience so your ad gets to the appropriate individuals. This is where Instagram ads flourish since you will be utilizing the demographic knowledge Facebook offers to get to the right individuals.

If you are using it for the first time, below are the targeting options you have at your disposal, which you can narrow down to reach a specific audience. For example, if you want to target men in Chicago between the ages of 18- 25, who are interested in sporting equipment, you will have the capacity to do that.

The targeting actions include:

- Location: Lets you target a city, state, country, or zip code and ignore specific areas.

- Gender: Pick between all genders, or only men/women.

- Age: Lets you target different age ranges.

- Demographics: You can access this under Detailed Targeting. It also has numerous sub-categories to pick from.

- Languages: Facebook suggests that you leave this place blank unless the language you want to target is not typical in the area you are aiming to target.

- Behaviors: This is also an option you will find under Detailed Targeting. It provides you with numerous categories to explore. It could either be anniversaries, purchasing behaviors, job roles, and a host of other options.

- Interests: Still another option you will have access to under Detailed Targeting, which offers numerous sub-categories to delve into. If you search for individuals interested in horror movies or beverages, you get these options and many more.

- Custom Audience: With this option, you will upload your contact list and target leads or clients you aim to upsell.

- Lookalike Audience: Here, Instagram gives you the chance to locate audiences who share lots of similarities to your other audiences.

- Connections: Here, you can target individuals connected to your app, page, or event.

After configuring your audience, Facebook offers a gauge to show you how broad or specific your audience is. You must take note of this because you want to choose a point where your audience is not too broad since it is not adequately targeted. You don't want it to be too narrow either, since you may be unable to reach a sufficient number of users.

Determine your Placements

The next step after targeting the demographic of your choice is to select your placement. This is vital if your campaign objectives are to show the ads on Instagram alone. If you decide to forgo this step, Facebook will show your ads on both platforms.

This can be positive, but if you have created content for Instagram specifically, you need to select "edit placements" and choose Instagram as your placement. You also have the option to choose if you would prefer the ads to show up on stories, feeds, or both.

Determine your Ad Schedule and Budget

Setting the budget for your ads is vital in determining how long your ads will run and how many people you will reach.

You can never be sure how much money you will need and how effective your ad will be, so it's good to pay close attention to the ads when they first start. What's more, you can decide to pause or stop your ads at any point if you believe your budget is not being apportioned the right way.

So, which should you go with, a daily or lifetime budget? This depends solely on you, but if you decide to go with a daily budget, it ensures your budget does not get exhausted fast. In contrast, a lifetime budget gives you the capacity for scheduling your ad delivery. Both options do the work they should, so it is a matter of choice.

Develop Your Instagram Ad
Here comes the moment you need to select your ad framework. Here, the set-up may seem different based on the objective you decide to go with.

There are six ad formats that Instagram provides you with. Two show up on Instagram stories, while the other four show up on your Instagram feed from the options provided below:

- Image Feed Ads: Most common ads and show up in the feed as an image.

- Image Story Ads: Image ads that show up in stories with captions.

- Video Feed Ads: Videos that play automatically while scrolling through the feed.

- Video Story Ads: These videos are displayed while users browse through their usual stories.

- Carousel Feed Ads: These allow you to put multiple images together.

- Canvas Feed Ads: A mobile ad that immerses the user in a full-screen experience for brands and businesses to showcase products.

Tips for Advertising on Instagram

Now that you understand the frameworks of ad creation, below are a few things to note when developing an ad that will ensure engagement:

Know Your Audience

When you have in-depth knowledge of who your audience is, what they like, and where they spend their time, you will be able to create messaging that they can instantly connect with.

Before you begin to run any ads, you should do your best to have as much information as you can on your target audience. Ask yourself:

- What are their wants and needs?

- What solution does your service or product provide to them?

- What are their values and goals?

- How can I best align my product/service to meet their requirements?

These questions should help you create the ideal marketing campaign for your chosen audience. Keep these in mind whenever you launch an ad campaign, and you'll be able to amplify your reach and effectiveness.

Chapter 6   Using Videos for Higher Engagements

Your Secret Weapon for Engagement, Generating Sales & Going Viral

One feature that gets a lot of attention on Instagram is people's ability to post videos to their account. Introduced in 2013, it quickly became a popular option, and there is no sign of that growth slowing down anytime soon.

Initially, there was a 15 second limit on the length of videos on Instagram. However, now videos can be up to a minute long. This provides users with an extended amount of customization options and promotion by editing videos and adding filters.

Already, many businesses and brands are beginning to use Instagram videos to engage with their fans and increase their follower base. People no longer have to spend their time on Facebook, Twitter, or YouTube to get access to content-packed videos. This is huge for those looking to take their Instagram game to the next level.

If you have spent any time on the internet, you probably know how powerful viral videos can be. On any social media platform that you look at, viral videos get an extraordinary number of engagements, comments, and shares.

It's important to remember that viral videos' success is measured by the number of views accumulated. On Instagram, views work a little differently. The video needs to be watched by the viewer for at least 3 seconds to be counted as a 'view.' If you have many viral videos on your account, you can expect significant long-term growth.

Videos sell, and that is not going to change anytime soon. Here are some tips to take advantage of this underrated Instagram strategy.:

- Choose a thumbnail that gets high engagement. When you post your video, the thumbnail will be the frozen image that previews part of the video. People will see this before clicking the video, meaning that you must capture their attention right away. Put the exciting stuff in front of their face!

- Choose videos that can potentially go viral and provide you with a high engagement rate: You want to pick videos that your audience can relate to while reaching out to potential followers. This is no different from the content strategy discussed earlier in this book. If you can do this consistently, you will see a lot of success with comments, likes, and most importantly, new followers.

- Make sure the highlight of the video happens right away. Unlike video sharing on other platforms, you can't skip to a specific part of a video on Instagram. You have to sit and watch the entire thing until the very end.

Creating videos takes more effort than posting a picture, but it is difficult to deny that they are a useful growth hack when used correctly and consistently. Videos are not mandatory and should only be used if they make sense in the context of your niche. With that being said, you will get better at making them over time as you practice and test new things out to see which videos get the highest levels of engagement.

Instagram has recently added a feature that allows you to go live, similar to Facebook's live streaming feature. The significant aspect of going live on Instagram is that Instagram notifies all your followers who are currently on Instagram and tells them you are live. This feature has not received much attention yet. However, it's still worthy of recognition since it provides a way for you to instantly share information and gain an instant response from your followers.

Now is the time to get ahead of the curve and begin taking advantage of the Instagram live feature. Connect with your followers and allow them to see you in real-time in your natural form. What do I mean? I mean, your followers should realize you're a real person, that you're not perfect, and that you are vulnerable enough to allow them to interact with you and your imperfect life.

Hack: Repurposing your Instagram live videos can be a great way to spread your content across other social media platforms. Instagram allows you to save your live videos. I highly encourage you to take advantage of this and make your videos available for your followers who didn't have the opportunity to watch you live.

Videos are by far the best way to communicate a message to your followers. Nothing conveys an idea and allows you to layout your services' benefits like a video will. I understand none of us are the best when we first start recording videos, and many of us are in the same boat. This makes it an excellent opportunity to get a head start on your competition and dictate the game.

When you learn to pitch your products and services using the 60-second timeframe Instagram gives you, you will not only see your follower base engage with you more than ever before, you'll also see your sales skyrocket.

Using IGTV to Increase Your Following

IGTV (Instagram Television) is a new and alternative way to engage your followers using videos. These videos stay in place for as long as you leave them up, which means that followers can look back through your IGTV channel and watch stuff that you put up days, weeks, months, or even years ago. (Once the feature has been around long enough).

You can leverage IGTV to create new followers by creating excellent IGTV videos and promoting them across other platforms. Increasing the likelihood of people tuning in to your channel and watching your video. Once they see your video and the quality you create, they can choose to follow your page to get more. The massive opportunity with IGTV is that you can promote your IGTV channel just like you would a YouTube channel.

This means that you can funnel people from Facebook, Twitter, Snapchat, email, and any other social media platform to Instagram, to enjoy your free content and learn from it. To make your content accessible, you need to make sure that the IGTV videos you make are worthy of receiving views. In other words, you need to create high-quality and engaging content.

The best way to create valuable content is to offer entertainment, insight, or guidance concerning your industry. For example, if you are an astrologer, you can create daily videos providing the day's astrological forecast. If you are a sports announcer, you can create a daily video highlighting the most memorable sports moment of the week or the latest stats of famous players or teams. If you are an educator, you can create a simple ten-minute or less tutorial on how your audience can do something for themselves that ties with your industry or your area of expertise.

By creating valuable content like this, you make it easier for your audience to understand why and how they are gaining value from your channel, which means that you will have an easier time promoting it and getting traction from that offer.

Once you have created fantastic content, make sure that you leverage it by sharing it across your other social media platforms, talking about it in your stories, writing about it in your latest post, and saving it for a future date.

When you create timeless content, you can always use it as a reference to older videos. For example, suppose you are a makeup artist and created a specific tutorial. In that case, you can promote the video as soon as you make it and then refer to it if you notice someone famous wore a similar look in a recent event. This is an excellent opportunity to create one piece of content with maximum impact, meaning that you can gain even more followers just from one ideal time investment. When it comes to marketing, that's what it's all about!

Instagram Stories: That Which You Need to Know

Instagram story is a feature that allows users to create videos and photos in a slide show format. These are like Snapchat stories that vanish after twenty-four hours, rather than an ordinary Instagram post (which only disappears if an individual or Instagram deletes it or moves it to archive).

Stories do not appear on a user's Instagram grid; they are signaled by a colored circle around an individual's profile picture.

Stories feature the exact light-hearted and enjoyable content as Snapchat, minus the requirement to create a new audience on still another social media platform. And, unlike conventional Instagram posts that could get lost on your viewer's feed, your Instagram stories are readily reachable, sitting directly at the top of the app.

Instagram stories can also be incredibly interactive. To dress them up, you're able to write or doodle on the pictures, set Instagram filters, tag users, and much more. You can even add a poll so that your audience can respond. Recently, Instagram rolled out another interactive feature, your audience's ability to ask you a question that you can then react to in your own Instagram story. In case your primary purpose is to participate with your crowd, then your chances are infinite.

Unlike a standard Instagram picture, you're able to view which users are seeing your Instagram story. If you upload more than one image or video, you can see whether they are clicking all the ways through and see what content is more engaging. This is a smooth quality, which will be hugely perceptive.

Say you submitted eight pictures on your own Instagram story; however, there is a considerable drop off in audiences going on to the next picture. You can very quickly return to the image and check what may have gone wrong. Can it be unexciting or potentially offensive? It's simple to analyze and correct your plan for the next round.

Instagram stories have proved valuable for users, influencers, and marketers alike. Audiences promptly adopted short-form videos and graphics. Proving once more that Instagram is committed to bringing the best features to the platform.

5 Methods to Utilize Instagram Stories for Business

You will find an assortment of strategies that you could use to get results with Instagram stories, every one of which can help your business in various ways.

1. Share content generated by your audience

2. Acquire content from your audience (Polls, Q&A quizzes, etc.)

3. Share moments from events

4. Be real - Use videos and images to inform your brand's narrative, throwing in particular behind the scene's content when available.

5. Go live (Feature other people)

Extending the Life Span of Stories with Highlights

Historically, stories disappeared after 24 hours, similar to the Snapchat feature these were emulating. Instagram realized this led to lost ROI on such content and updated us with the ability to create highlights. Highlights are featured on our profile page, and we can add Stories to them after their 24 hours of glory have been given.

You can create multiple Highlights on your page, each with a unique story to tell. For unique features about yourself, you might label one "About Me," and for a recent event, "Seminar 2020." This tends to make it a lot easier for users to locate articles they are searching for once they come to your profile and allows them to get to know you a little faster.

Now that we've covered all of the essential details to get started, build your account, and engage your followers, it's time to move on to ways you can monetize your account and reap the benefits of your hard work.

Chapter 7   Different Ways to Make Money on Instagram

One of the advantages of using Instagram is that there are multiple ways you can earn money through the platform. While most of this guidebook has focused on how you can grow your following and gain customers, these indispensable building blocks are the foundation for monetizing your online reach.

A business may decide to sell their own products online and profit that way, but what about the people who don't have a product or service?

There are many other methods businesses and individuals can earn a nice income online, from all the hard work done to gain followers and a good reputation. Let's take a look at some of the different ways that you can make money on Instagram.

Affiliate Marketing

The first option is to work as an affiliate marketer. With this model, you promote a product for a company and then get paid a commission for each sale. This model is popular with influencers because they work on growing their audience, writing articles, posting product reviews, vlogging about a product that their audience is interested in, and making money on any sales through affiliate links.

To be an affiliate marketer on Instagram, you would need to post attractive images of products you choose and drive sales through your affiliate URL. You will get this affiliate link through the company you choose to advertise with. Just make sure that you are going with an affiliate that offers high-quality products, so you don't send your followers inferior products. And check that you earn a decent commission on each one.

Once you get your affiliate URL, add it to the captions of the posts you are promoting and, in the bio, since you can't click on the caption link. You can use www.bitly.com to shorten the address or customize your affiliate link.

If you have a good following on Instagram already, then this method of making money can be pretty straightforward. You just need to find a product that goes with your page's theme and then advertise it to your customers. Ensure that the product is high-quality so that your customers are happy with the recommendations you give.

Here's a list of affiliates you can check out to get started:

- ShareASale Affiliates.
- Solvid Affiliate.
- **Amazon** Associates.
- **eBay** Partners.
- Shopify Affiliate Program.
- Clickbank.
- Rakuten Marketing Affiliates.
- Leadpages Partner Program.

Sell Pictures

This one may seem obvious, but it can be an excellent way for photographers to showcase some of the work they have. If you are an amateur or professional photographer, you will find that Instagram is the perfect way to advertise and even sell your shots. You can choose to sell your services to big agencies or even to individuals who may need pictures for their websites or marketing.

When posting pictures you want to sell on your profile, make sure each one has a watermark. This makes it hard for customers to take the images without paying you first. You can also use captions to list the terms of selling pictures, so there isn't any confusion.

To make this work, take time to keep your presence on Instagram active. This ensures that the right people and the best accounts are exposed to your content. Using the right hashtags for your shots comes in good hands for this, helping people find your photographs quickly. You may even want to take the time to get some engagement and conversations started with big agencies in the photography world who can help you grow even more.

Sell Advertising Space on Your Page (Shoutouts)

If you have a large enough following, you could get individuals, brands, and companies interested in buying advertising space on your profile. They will use this to gain access to your followers to increase their followers, sell a product, or increase brand awareness. This is the perfect and most common approach for making money from all the hard work in growing your page.

There are many different ways that you can do this. You can offer to let them send a video, which you post on your story, promote a picture on your profile, or use any other ad/shoutout format. You can then charge for the type of service they decide to use, the amount of time they want to advertise for, and how big of an audience you are promoting them in front of.

You can list your service online at Shoutcart, or you can let people know through your bio. (DM for promotions, collaborations, etc.)

Become a Brand Ambassador

This is something that is becoming popular with MLM companies. There is so much competition on Twitter and Facebook that many are turning to Instagram as a new way to promote their products and get followers they may not have reached through other means. Because of Instagram's visual aspects, these ambassadors can showcase the products through pictures and videos.

There are many companies that you can choose from when it comes to being a brand ambassador. Since you have already taken some time to build up your audience and you have a good following, you can now find a good company that produces excellent products/services and work with them consistently.

You can advertise these products and services to your followers without having the headache of running your own business and make a fair amount of money. However, you have to pick out a company with products/services your followers will enjoy, ones that go with your profile's theme to enhance your profits and maintain authenticity.

Promote Your Services, Products, or Business

Finally, if you already run a business, then Instagram can be an excellent way to market, promote, and engage with your customers. Here are a few ways you can promote your business through Instagram:

•Behind the scenes content: These are very popular on Instagram. Show your followers what it takes to make the products you sell. Show them some of your employees working. Show something that the follower usually won't see because it is unique and makes them feel like they are part of your inner circle.

•Pictures from your customers: If you pick out the right hashtag and share it with your customers, they will start to use it with some of their pictures. You can then use this content to help promote your business even more.

•Exclusive offers and infographics: You can take the time to market your services through Instagram with some exclusive offers and infographics of your products. This works well if the deals are ones the customer wouldn't be able to find anywhere else.

As you can see, there are many different options that you can choose from when you want to make some money through your Instagram account.

All of the methods can be used no matter what your interests are. After you build your audience and have many followers looking at your profile and engaging with your content, you can leverage this to make money on Instagram.

Remember, 70% of your post should be used to reach new people, 20% to build trust, and 10% to generate sales. This makes sure your page is always growing, and you maintain your audience's goodwill, which will make them want to support you through buying what you have on offer.

Conclusion

Thank you for reading The Ultimate Instagram Guide. We hope you found all the information and tools you need to achieve your goals. But remember, knowledge is only potential power till you put it to use.

The next step is to get online and use all the information in this book to grow your account. If you already have a personal account, it is best to start one that is just for business or switch to a creator account to obtain the metrics you need regarding your page.

Once that is done, it is time to start posting high-quality pictures to show off your products and services, reach out to potential customers, and bring out your presence on Instagram.

This guidebook spent some time looking at the benefits of using Instagram marketing and why you would want to choose this for growing your business.

In the end, we covered how to leverage these skills to bring in paying customers.

We wish you the best of success on your journey and hope to see your content soon!

Printed in Great Britain
by Amazon

25841090R00036